HAL•LEONARD®
PIANO PLAY-ALONG

AUDIO
ACCESS
INCLUDED

PLAYBACK+
Speed • Pitch • Balance • Loop

69

ISBN 978-1-4234-6154-8

Disney characters and artwork © Disney Enterprises, Inc.

WALT DISNEY MUSIC COMPANY

DISTRIBUTED BY

7777 W. BLUEMOUND RD. P.O. BOX 13819 MILWAUKEE, WI 53213

In Australia Contact:
Hal Leonard Australia Pty. Ltd.
4 Lentara Court
Cheltenham, Victoria, 3192 Australia
Email: ausadmin@halleonard.com.au

Visit Hal Leonard Online at
www.halleonard.com

CONTENTS

PAGE	TITLE

THE BLACK PEARL

from Walt Disney Pictures' PIRATES OF THE CARIBBEAN: THE CURSE OF THE BLACK PEARL

Music by KLAUS BADELT

Quickly, in 1

8

DAVY JONES

from Walt Disney Pictures' PIRATES OF THE CARIBBEAN: DEAD MAN'S CHEST

Music by HANS ZIMMER

Tempo I

Both hands 8va

L.H.

p

(8va)

(8va)

(loco)

(8va)

HE'S A PIRATE

from Walt Disney Pictures' PIRATES OF THE CARIBBEAN: THE CURSE OF THE BLACK PEARL

Music by KLAUS BADELT

Briskly

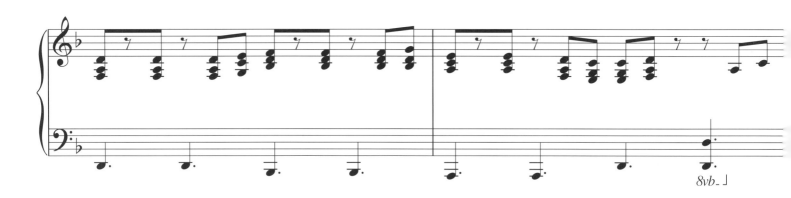

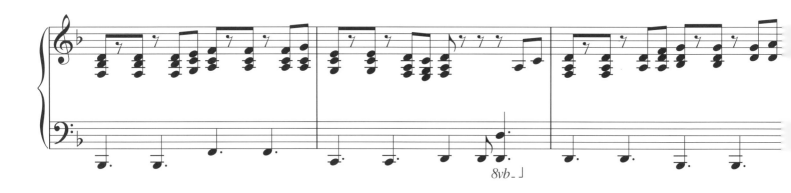

I'VE GOT MY EYE ON YOU

from Walt Disney Pictures' PIRATES OF THE CARIBBEAN: DEAD MAN'S CHEST

Music by HANS ZIMMER

JACK SPARROW

from Walt Disney Pictures' PIRATES OF THE CARIBBEAN: DEAD MAN'S CHEST

Music by HANS ZIMMER

Moderately slow

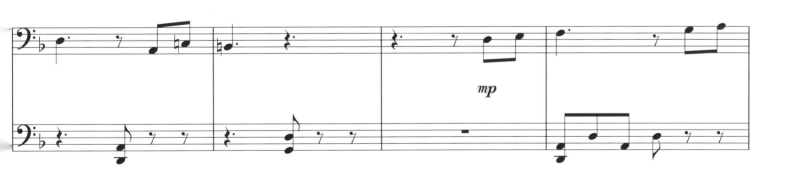

THE MEDALLION CALLS

from Walt Disney Pictures' PIRATES OF THE CARIBBEAN: THE CURSE OF THE BLACK PEARL

Music by KLAUS BADELT

THE KRAKEN

from Walt Disney Pictures' PIRATES OF THE CARIBBEAN: DEAD MAN'S CHEST

Music by HANS ZIMMER

Slow and steady

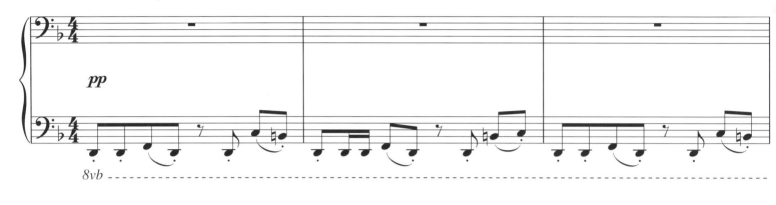

With pedal

TWO HORNPIPES
(Fisher's Hornpipe)
from Walt Disney Pictures' PIRATES OF THE CARIBBEAN: DEAD MAN'S CHEST

By SKIP HENDERSON

THE ULTIMATE SONGBOOKS

HAL•LEONARD®
PIANO PLAY-ALONG

AUDIO ACCESS INCLUDED

These great songbooks come with our standard arrangements for piano and voice with guitar chord frames plus audio.

Each book includes either a CD or access to online recordings of full performance of each song, as well as a second track without the piano part so you can play "lead" with the band!

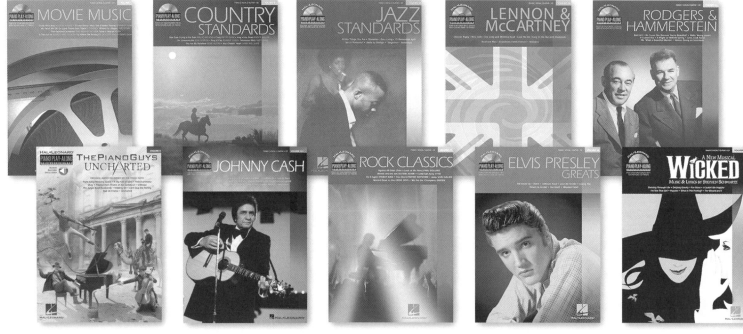

71. GEORGE GERSHWIN
00102687 P/V/G $24.99

72. VAN MORRISON
00103053 P/V/G $14.99

73. MAMMA MIA! – THE MOVIE
00311831 P/V/G $15.99

76. PRIDE & PREJUDICE
00311862 P/V/G $14.99

77. ELTON JOHN FAVORITES
00311884 P/V/G $14.99

78. ERIC CLAPTON
00311885 P/V/G $14.99

79. TANGOS
00311886 P/V/G $14.99

80. FIDDLER ON THE ROOF
00311887 P/V/G $14.99

81. JOSH GROBAN
00311901 P/V/G $14.99

82. LIONEL RICHIE
00311902 P/V/G $14.99

83. PHANTOM OF THE OPERA
00311903 P/V/G $15.99

84. ANTONIO CARLOS JOBIM FAVORITES
00311919 P/V/G $14.99

85. LATIN FAVORITES
00311920 P/V/G $14.99

86. BARRY MANILOW
00311935 P/V/G $14.99

87. PATSY CLINE
00311936 P/V/G $14.99

88. NEIL DIAMOND
00311937 P/V/G $14.99

89. FAVORITE HYMNS
00311940 P/V/G $14.99

90. IRISH FAVORITES
00311969 P/V/G $14.99

92. DISNEY FAVORITES
00311973 P/V/G $14.99

93. THE TWILIGHT SAGA:
NEW MOON – SOUNDTRACK
00311974 P/V/G $16.99

95. TAYLOR SWIFT
00311984 P/V/G $14.99

96. BEST OF LENNON & MCCARTNEY
00311996 P/V/G $14.99

97. GREAT CLASSICAL THEMES
00312020 PIANO SOLO $14.99

98. CHRISTMAS CHEER
00312021 P/V/G $14.99

99. ANTONIO CARLOS JOBIM CLASSICS
00312039 P/V/G $14.99

100. COUNTRY CLASSICS
00312041 P/V/G $14.99

103. GOSPEL FAVORITES
00312044 P/V/G $14.99

105. BEE GEES
00312055 P/V/G $14.99

106. CAROLE KING
00312056 P/V/G $14.99

107. BOB DYLAN
00312057 P/V/G $16.99

108. SIMON & GARFUNKEL
00312058 P/V/G $16.99

111. STEVIE WONDER
00312119 P/V/G $14.99

112. JOHNNY CASH
00312156 P/V/G $14.99

113. QUEEN
00312164 P/V/G $16.99

114. MOTOWN
00312176 P/V/G $14.99

115. JOHN DENVER
00312249 P/V/G $14.99

116. JAMIE CULLUM
00312275 P/V/G $14.99

117. ALICIA KEYS
00312306 P/V/G $14.99

118. ADELE
00312307 P/V/G $14.99

121. NORAH JONES
00306559 P/V/G $19.99

122. WORSHIP HITS
00312564 P/V/G $14.99

123. CHRIS TOMLIN
00312563 P/V/G $14.99

124. WINTER WONDERLAND
00101872 P/V/G $14.99

125. KATY PERRY
00109373 P/V/G $14.99

126. BRUNO MARS
00123121 P/V/G $14.99

127. STAR WARS
00110282 PIANO SOLO $14.99

128. FROZEN
00126480 P/V/G $14.99

130. WEST SIDE STORY
00130738 P/V/G $14.99

131. THE PIANO GUYS – WONDERS*
00141503 P/V/G $24.99

132. TODAY'S HITS
00147793 P/V/G $14.99

Visit Hal Leonard Online at
www.halleonard.com

Prices, contents and availability
subject to change without notice.

PEANUTS © United Feature Syndicate, Inc.
Disney characters and artwork © Disney Enterprises, Inc.

* Audio contains backing tracks only.

YOUR FAVORITE MUSIC
ARRANGED FOR PIANO SOLO

ADELE FOR PIANO SOLO – 2ND EDITION
This collection features 13 Adele favorites beautifully arranged for piano solo, including: Chasing Pavements • Hello • Rolling in the Deep • Set Fire to the Rain • Someone like You • Turning Tables • When We Were Young • and more.
00307585 ....$12.99

PRIDE & PREJUDICE
12 piano pieces from the 2006 Oscar-nominated film, including: Another Dance • Darcy's Letter • Georgiana • Leaving Netherfield • Liz on Top of the World • Meryton Townhall • The Secret Life of Daydreams • Stars and Butterflies • and more.
00313327 ....$17.99

BATTLESTAR GALACTICA
by Bear McCreary
For this special collection, McCreary himself has translated the acclaimed orchestral score into fantastic solo piano arrangements at the intermediate to advanced level. Includes 19 selections in all, and as a bonus, simplified versions of "Roslin and Adama" and "Wander My Friends." Contains a note from McCreary, as well as a biography.
00313530 ....$17.99

GEORGE GERSHWIN – RHAPSODY IN BLUE (ORIGINAL)
Alfred Publishing Co.
George Gershwin's own piano solo arrangement of his classic contemporary masterpiece for piano and orchestra. This masterful measure-for-measure two-hand adaptation of the complete modern concerto for piano and orchestra incorporates all orchestral parts and piano passages into two staves while retaining the clarity, sonority, and brilliance of the original.
00321589 ....$16.99

THE BEST JAZZ PIANO SOLOS EVER
Over 300 pages of beautiful classic jazz piano solos featuring standards in any jazz artist's repertoire. Includes: Afternoon in Paris • Giant Steps • Moonlight in Vermont • Moten Swing • A Night in Tunisia • Night Train • On Green Dolphin Street • Song for My Father • West Coast Blues • Yardbird Suite • and more.
00312079 ....$19.99

ROMANTIC FILM MUSIC
40 piano solo arrangements of beloved songs from the silver screen, including: Anyone at All • Come What May • Glory of Love • I See the Light • I Will Always Love You • Iris • It Had to Be You • Nobody Does It Better • She • Take My Breath Away (Love Theme) • A Thousand Years • Up Where We Belong • When You Love Someone • The Wind Beneath My Wings • and many more.
00122112 ....$17.99

CLASSICS WITH A TOUCH OF JAZZ
Arranged by Lee Evans
27 classical masterpieces arranged in a unique and accessible jazz style. Mr Evans also provides an audio recording of each piece. Titles include: Air from Suite No. 3 (Bach) • Barcarolle "June" (Tchaikovsky) • Pavane (Faure) • Piano Sonata No. 8 "Pathetique" (Beethoven) • Reverie (Debussy) • The Swan (Saint-Saens) • and more.
00151662 Book/Online Audio...$14.99

STAR WARS: THE FORCE AWAKENS
Music from the soundtrack to the seventh installment of the Star Wars® franchise by John Williams is presented in this songbook, complete with artwork from the film throughout the whole book, including eight pages in full color! Titles include: The Scavenger • Rey Meets BB-8 • Rey's Theme • That Girl with the Staff • Finn's Confession • The Starkiller • March of the Resistance • Torn Apart • and more.
00154451 ....$17.99

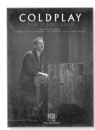

COLDPLAY FOR PIANO SOLO
Stellar solo arrangements of a dozen smash hits from Coldplay: Clocks • Fix You • In My Place • Lost! • Paradise • The Scientist • Speed of Sound • Trouble • Up in Flames • Viva La Vida • What If • Yellow.
00307637 ....$15.99

TAYLOR SWIFT FOR PIANO SOLO – 2ND EDITION
This updated second edition features 15 of Taylor's biggest hits from her self-titled first album all the way through her pop breakthrough album, *1989*. Includes: Back to December • Blank Space • Fifteen • I Knew You Were Trouble • Love Story • Mean • Mine • Picture to Burn • Shake It Off • Teardrops on My Guitar • 22 • We Are Never Ever Getting Back Together • White Horse • Wildest Dreams • You Belong with Me.
00307375 ....$16.99

DISNEY SONGS
12 Disney favorites in beautiful piano solo arrangements, including: Bella Notte (This Is the Night) • Can I Have This Dance • Feed the Birds • He's a Tramp • I'm Late • The Medallion Calls • Once Upon a Dream • A Spoonful of Sugar • That's How You Know • We're All in This Together • You Are the Music in Me • You'll Be in My Heart (Pop Version).
00313527 ....$14.99

UP
Music by Michael Giacchino
Piano solo arrangements of 13 pieces from Pixar's mammoth animated hit: Carl Goes Up • It's Just a House • Kevin Beak'n • Married Life • Memories Can Weigh You Down • The Nickel Tour • Paradise Found • The Small Mailman Returns • The Spirit of Adventure • Stuff We Did • We're in the Club Now • and more, plus a special section of full-color artwork from the film!
00313471 ....$16.99

GREAT THEMES FOR PIANO SOLO
Nearly 30 rich arrangements of popular themes from movies and TV shows, including: Bella's Lullaby • Chariots of Fire • Cinema Paradiso • The Godfather (Love Theme) • Hawaii Five-O Theme • Theme from "Jaws" • Theme from "Jurassic Park" • Linus and Lucy • The Pink Panther • Twilight Zone Main Title • and more.
00312102 ....$14.99

Prices, content, and availability subject to change without notice.
Disney Characters and Artwork TM & © 2018 Disney

HAL•LEONARD®
7777 W. BLUEMOUND RD. P.O. BOX 13819 MILWAUKEE, WI 53213
www.halleonard.com